The Longest Journey

The Story of the Donner Party

by Cynthia Mercati

HAMLIN ROBINSON SCHOOL
10211 12th Ave. S.
Seattle, WA 98168

Perfection Learning®

Cover Illustration: Dan Hatala
Inside Illustration: Dan Hatala pp 17, 22, 33, 48; Dea Marks p 9 (bottom)

About the Author

Cynthia Mercati is a writer and a professional actress. She has written many plays for a children's theatre that tours and performs at various schools. She also appears in many of the plays herself.

Ms. Mercati loves reading about history and visiting historical places. When she writes a historical play or book, she wants her readers to feel like they are actually living the story.

Ms. Mercati also loves baseball. Her favorite team is the Chicago White Sox. She grew up in Chicago, Illinois, but she now lives in Des Moines, Iowa. Ms. Mercati has two children and one dog.

Image credits:
© **California State Parks, 2001,** p. 5 Patty Reed, p. 44 Sutter's Fort, p. 55 Replica of Patty Reed's Doll; Courtesy of the **Bancroft Library**, University of California, Berkeley, p. 28 Camp on Donner Lake (BANC MSS C-B 570), p. 43 Arrival of Relief Party (BANC MSS C-B 570), p. 53 Dedication of Pioneer Monument (BANC MSS C-B 570); Used by permission, **Utah State Historical Society**, all rights reserved, p. 11 Lansford Hastings (12483), p. 6 James Reed Frazier (13371); Special Collections, **J. Willard Marriott Library**, University of Utah, p. 44 William Henry Eddy (P0100 #18), p. 14 Eleanor Priscilla Eddy (P0100 #17); Reproduced by permission of **The Huntington Library**, San Marino, California, p. 14 Lewis Keseberg, p. 29 W. C. Graves, p. 29 Mary A. Graves, p. 41 Virginia E. Reed

ArtToday (some images copyright www.arttoday.com) pp 4, 9 (top), 10, 11 (top), 13, 15, 18, 20, 21, 24, 30, 34, 36, 37, 38, 40, 47; Art Explosion® p 35; Corel Professional Photos pp 25, 26–27

Printed in the United States of America. For information, contact Perfection Learning® Corporation, 1000 North Second Avenue, P.O. Box 500, Logan, Iowa 51546-0500.
Tel: 1-800-831-4190 • Fax: 1-800-543-2745
PB ISBN-13: 978-0-7891-5615-0 ISBN-10: 0-7891-5615-6
RLB ISBN-13: 978-0-7569-0426-5 ISBN-10: 0-7569-0426-9

4 5 6 7 8 9 PP 12 11 10 09 08 07

Contents

Chapter

The Beginning

It was April 15, 1846. Three families were ready for the trip from Springfield, Illinois, to California. They were the James Reed family, the George Donner family, and the Jacob Donner family. George and Jacob were brothers.

The families would travel in covered wagons. Later, they would be known as the Donner party.

Many stories have been told about the Donner party. Some are true. Some are not.

But the story I'm about to tell you is all true. I'm Patty Reed. I was one of the children with the Donner party.

Patty Reed as an adult

I was eight years old when we left for California. My life in Springfield had been very happy.

Patty's mother and father, James and Margaret Reed

My father was James Reed. He owned a furniture business. We lived in a big house and were well-off.

But my father liked adventure. He was always making big plans.

In 1846, California belonged to Mexico. The Mexican government wanted people to settle in California. They were selling land for very little money.

My father wanted some of that land. He wanted to build a big farm and a big ranch.

My mother didn't want to go west. She was often ill with bad headaches. She thought the trip would be too hard for her. But when Papa made up his mind about something, he stuck to it.

Papa had a special wagon built for us. He called it the "Pioneer Palace Car." It had a stove, beds, and padded seats. He said it was a palace on wheels.

We had two other wagons as well. One was for food and supplies. The other was for all the things we'd need in California.

Our wagons were pulled by teams of oxen. Papa hired some young men to walk beside the oxen and guide them. These men were called *teamsters*.

Papa also hired a servant for my mother. Her name was Eliza Williams. She would help Mother with the chores along the trail.

Papa and my sister, Virginia, would ride horses. Virginia was almost 13. She liked to have adventures, just like our father.

My grandmother, Mama, and I would ride inside the wagon. My two brothers, Jimmy and Tommy, would ride inside too. Jimmy was five. Tommy was three.

George and Tamsen Donner had five children. Jacob and Elizabeth Donner had seven children. I'd have lots of friends to play with.

We couldn't leave our dogs behind! There were five of them. Barney, Tyler, Tracker, Trailer, and Cash. Cash was our special pet.

Our neighbors came to see us off. It was hard to leave them. It was hard to leave our old home and all we had ever known.

Holding my special doll close to my heart made me feel better. She had black hair and a china face.

Finally, our nine wagons started off.

"Good-bye!" everyone called out. "Good luck!"

"We won't need luck," Papa said. "We're ready for anything that might happen!"

Chapter

2

The Lie

In 1846, only a few hundred Americans lived in California. It took a long time to get there.

But my father and the Donner brothers thought they had found a shorter way to get there. The route was described in a book called *The Emigrants' Guide to Oregon and California.* Lansford Hastings was the author.

Lansford Hastings

11

Hastings wrote that folks bound for California should leave the regular trail at Fort Hall. Then they should head southwest. He said hundreds of miles would be saved.

There was just one problem. Hastings had never seen the cutoff he'd written about. He was just guessing it was there. But the people in our wagon train didn't know that.

In 1842, Hastings had been given land in California. He wanted lots of people to go there so he could sell his land. He thought that if he said there was a quicker way to get there, more settlers would want to go.

We believed in Lansford Hastings. We believed in his shortcut.

We didn't know our great trip to California was based on a lie.

Chapter 3

The Vote

We reached Independence, Missouri, in May. There, the Breen family joined our little wagon train. They had seven children. The youngest was only a year old.

On May 29, we had our first sadness on the trail. My grandmother died.

My father and brothers dug a grave for her under a tree. Mother snipped a lock of Grandmother's hair. She folded it inside a handkerchief.

As we buried Grandma, my mother wept hard tears. Virginia and I cried too. I held my doll close.

Our wagons rolled on west. We headed into Nebraska. The weather turned dry. The only trees were cottonwoods. They grew along the banks of the Platte River.

Other families joined our train. The Murphys, the Eddys, the Graveses, the Stantons, and the Kesebergs.

Lewis Keseberg

The Kesebergs were from Germany. Mr. Keseberg and Papa did not get along.

Lewis Keseberg was jealous of our big Palace Car. He was jealous of our money. He told people that Papa put on airs.

Eleanor Eddy

By the second week of July, we

reached Independence Rock in Wyoming. It stood 200 feet high. We all scratched our names on the granite surface.

On July 20, we crossed through a pass in the Rocky Mountains. We came down the trail to Little Sandy Creek. There, we had to take a vote.

Should we stay on the regular trail? Or take the cutoff?

Only the men and the boys over the age of 14 were allowed to vote. They decided to leave the trail.

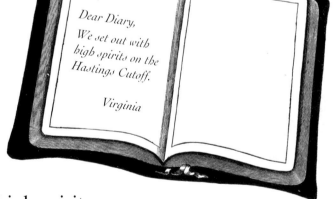

Virginia was keeping a diary. On July 31, she wrote, ". . . we set out with high spirits on the Hastings Cutoff."

Our high spirits would not last long.

July 31

Dear Diary,

We set out with high spirits on the Hastings Cutoff.

Virginia

The Cutoff

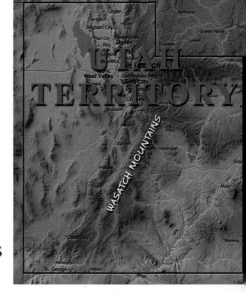

We soon crossed into the Wasatch Mountains. In his guidebook, Hastings had said there would be a trail to follow.

He was wrong.

The men used picks and axes to cut a path through the thick trees. They pried up big boulders with crowbars.

They lowered the wagons down the mountain walls on ropes, one at a time. Then they had to pull the wagons up again on the other side.

By the end of August, we made it through the mountains. But waiting for us was the Great Salt Lake Desert.

The sun baked us during the day. At night, we shivered with cold. Dust burned our skin.

Hastings had said it would take us only two days and two nights to cross the desert. He was wrong again.

No one rode anymore, not even Mama. But the oxen still had a hard time pulling the wagons. We had to lighten their load.

We threw out our beautiful dishes and furniture. We tossed out our books and our toys.

I was scared Mother was going to make me leave my doll behind. I hid her inside my dress.

18

After three days, everyone was out of water. All but two of our family's oxen had dropped dead of thirst.

I felt so sad. I wanted to cry. But I was too dry. No tears would come.

We hitched up the two last oxen to the Palace Car. We had to leave our other two wagons behind.

Finally, we reached water.

On September 26, we came to the Humboldt River. This was where the cutoff rejoined the main trail to California.

But our shortcut had cost us extra time. We were a month behind all the other wagon trains.

We all knew what that meant. We were now in danger of getting caught in a snowstorm in the Sierra Nevada.

5
Chapter

The Good-bye

By September, our food supplies were running low. We were all hungry and tired. Tempers were growing short.

One morning, we started up a steep sand hill. Our oxen got tangled up with the oxen from another wagon. Two teamsters started shouting at each other.

The teamster from the other wagon was named John Snyder. He started lashing our two oxen with his whip.

Father ran over to Snyder.

"Ease up!" Father shouted.

"Get out of my way! Or I'll whip you too!" Snyder yelled back.

Angrily, Papa pulled out his hunting knife.

When Snyder saw that, he exploded. He cracked my father across the head with the butt of his whip. It dug into Father's skull. Blood gushed.

Father jumped at Snyder. He drove his knife into Snyder's chest.

John Snyder fell to the ground. He was dead.

Lewis Keseberg grabbed a rope.

"James Reed is a murderer!" he shouted. "He should be hung!"

Mother cried out. "No, no! Have mercy!"

The other men voted on Papa's punishment. He wouldn't be hung. But he would have to leave the wagon train.

One by one, our family hugged Papa. Mama was crying as if she would never stop.

Father mounted his horse. Then he leaned down for a last good-bye.

There were tears in his eyes too.

"Be brave," Papa whispered. "I promise you that we will all be together in California!"

I watched Papa ride away. I felt as if my heart would break. Tears fell down my cheeks. They spilled onto my doll.

Mother was told to leave our Palace Car behind. The men said it was slowing everyone down.

The Graves family let us move our few things into their wagon.

As the wagon train started off again, I looked back at our Palace Car.

Once it had been beautiful. Now it sat by the side of the road, dusty and broken.

I looked up at my mother's face. When we'd left Springfield, she'd been beautiful too. Now she looked old and worn.

Mama had lost her home, her mother, and her husband. Now most of her belongings were gone too.

"Mama," I whispered. "What are we going to do?"

"We just have to keep going," she said. "There is nothing else to do."

Chapter

The Pass

By mid-October we were climbing the Sierra Nevada.

The Native Americans said the mountains were "rock upon rock."

They were right.

Sharp winds blew across the steep cliffs. High peaks seemed to touch the sky. The mountains were like a wall, cutting us off from California. They cut us off from food and warmth.

Snow was already falling in the mountains. The higher we climbed, the deeper the snow was.

We divided into three groups. My family was in the second group. The Donner families made up the third group.

For several days, we struggled upward.

On October 31, the first group reached Truckee Lake. It was only a quarter of a mile below the pass that was our doorway to California!

But a solid wall of snow blocked our path to that doorway.

The first group found a small cabin. They stopped there to rest.

On November 1, my family arrived at the cabin. It was twilight. We were all dead tired. We told the others that the Donners had fallen far behind.

The next morning, we started out again. We yoked the few oxen we had left to our last few wagons. With all our might, we tried to make it to the pass.

That night, we slept on a bed of snow. More snow fell during the night.

By morning, the wind had whipped the new snow into high peaks. We left the wagons behind. We strapped what food we had left to the oxen's backs. We tried again to make it to the pass.

It was hopeless.

We couldn't go back down and we couldn't go ahead.

We had to face the fact that we were trapped in the mountains. For how long, we didn't know.

The first thing we had to do was find shelter.

Mr. Breen claimed the cabin for his family. He said he'd seen it first, so it was his. He sounded like a little child yelling "finders keepers!"

The Kesebergs built a three-wall shack against one end of the cabin.

The Graves family and our family chopped down trees. We built a new cabin. We put a wall down the middle.

Mary
Graves

Our family would
live on one side. The
Graves family would
live on the other side.
Several other families
built a large cabin to
share.

The Donners never
caught up with us. They
had to camp at Alder
Creek, six miles back.

After we built our
shelters, we killed the few
oxen that were left. We
used their hides to roof our
cabins. We put their meat in the
snow to freeze.

W. C.
Graves

Some of the men decided to go hunting.
But most of the animals had gone into the
lower mountains for the winter. The trout in
the lake weren't biting.

After three days of trying, the men bagged only one owl and a skinny coyote.

The men wouldn't be able to go out hunting again. The snow was starting to rise higher than our cabins. I hugged my doll close.

What would become of us?

Chapter

The Surprise

Everyone kept saying the same thing. "If only . . ."

"If only we'd left one day earlier, we could have made it across the pass."

"If only we hadn't taken the shortcut, we wouldn't have been caught in the snow."

Mama gathered all her children together. She ordered us to stop saying "If only . . ." She told us we were done with the past.

"Our job now is to figure out a way to stay alive," Mama said. "We must make it out of these mountains and be with Papa again!"

Mama's voice was firm. Her eyes were snapping. Her courage gave us courage.

But staying alive proved to be a very hard task.

Mama cut the leftover ox hides into strips. She burned off the hair.

Next, she boiled the strips and made soup. It looked like sticky glue. It tasted so bad we almost gagged. But we had to eat it. After the oxen meat was gone, it was all we had.

Then on Christmas, Mama gave us a surprise. On the day we'd built our cabin, Mama had hidden food deep in the snow.

"I decided I was going to give my children a good holiday no matter what," she told us.

On that day, we each had a handful of beans, half a cup of rice, a few dried apple slices, and a small square of bacon. We even had a helping of stew. Mama had made it from the oxen's stomach linings.

Back in Springfield, it wouldn't have even been a snack. But on that Christmas, it was more than a meal. It was a miracle!

8
Chapter

The Promise

By New Year's Eve, we didn't even have any ox hides left.

Mama trapped the mice that came into our cabin and cooked those.

She put ice in our cups and told us to shut our eyes. "Pretend it's ice cream!" she told us.

We tried our best.

Four of our dogs had died along the trail.

We still had Cash. But soon he, too, died.

Crying, Mama boiled up Cash's thin little body. The rest of us were crying too.

We ate every part of Cash's body. Even his feet and hide. Then Mama boiled down his bones for us to chew on.

"I think Cash would be happy to know he kept us alive for a few more days," Mama said.

The other families were eating equally horrible things to stay alive.

The Murphys cut a rug into pieces. They toasted each piece in front of the fire.

They told us that the crispy bits of rug went down easier than ox-hide soup.

Finally, Mama made a brave decision. "I'm going to try to cross the mountains," she said. "I have to get us some food!"

Mama said my brothers and I were too small to go. She told me to look after Jimmy and Tommy.

On January 4, 1847, she and Virginia started out. They were wearing homemade snowshoes. Milt went with them. He was one of our teamsters. Eliza went too.

The next day, Eliza stumbled back to camp. Mama and the others came back four days later. They were half dead from cold and hunger.

Virginia's feet were frostbitten. She had had to crawl back to camp on her hands and knees.

Mama started taking down pieces of hide from our roof. She boiled these for soup.

But soon those hides were gone too. Then we had nothing to eat.

We had no covering on our side of the cabin.

Thank goodness, the Breen family took us in.

The Breens still had food stored away. Every day, Mrs. Breen slipped Mama a little bit from their supplies. When Mr. Breen found out, he was very angry.

"Our food is for our family!" he shouted.

Mr. Breen did give Mama the bones from their meat. She boiled them over and over. She added anything she thought we could swallow—twigs, leaves, bark.

Mama did everything she could think of to keep us alive. She tried hard to keep our spirits up too.

When we'd been rich and comfortable, Mama had been sick much of the time. But now she was the healthiest of all of us. It was as if she was forcing herself to be strong for us.

Every night, Mama had us kneel down next to her by the fire. She read to us from the Bible. Every night, we prayed for Papa. We prayed to be rescued.

But every day, our hopes grew less and less.

So many people had already died of hunger and cold.

One night, Mr. Breen told us that some of the other families were living off the flesh of the dead. My two little brothers didn't understand what that meant.

But Virginia and I understood all too well. We looked at each other with dread. It was too horrible to think of. But we couldn't stop thinking of it.

Weak, horrified tears slipped down our cheeks.

Mama put her arms around my sister and me. Firmly she said, "Put it out of your mind. We will never do that! Never! I promise you. It's not right."

The Waiting

By February, we spent most of our time in a hungry daze. We were often too weak to sit up. We just lay in front of the fire.

Our windowless little cabin was dark, even during the day. The smell of unwashed bodies and clothes and the boiling bones was terrible.

One day, Virginia turned her head to me. "Patty," she whispered, "I feel myself slipping away. I feel like I'm going to fall asleep. And I'll never wake up again in this world."

Virginia

"Please don't say that, Virginia," I begged her. "Please try to hang on!"

Virginia said she would try. We were all trying to live just one more day.

But how much longer could we go on?

I would dream at night and during the day. My dreams were always the same.

I was back in Springfield. I was where it was warm and my stomach was full. And Papa was with us.

Then I'd wake up. I'd feel the sharp pains of hunger again. I'd feel the cold.

To keep myself from crying, I held my doll close to me. She was the last little bit of home I had left.

I felt like a starving animal, hiding in a dark cave. We were all like animals now, just waiting . . .

But what were we waiting for? Life or death?

Chapter

The Rescue

On December 16, 1846, five women and ten men had started out across the mountains. They were determined to bring us help. William Eddy was the leader.

Eight people died along the trail. The others made it to a Native American village. The Indians fed them.

William

Eddy kept going. His feet were frostbitten and bleeding. So he dragged himself along the snow-packed trail.

Finally, Eddy came to a ranch.

From there he sent a letter to Sutter's Fort in Sacramento, California. In the letter, he begged for a rescue party to go into the mountains.

Sutter's Fort

On February 18, 1847, that rescue party made it to our camp.

Everyone came crawling out of the cabins. Some of us cried. Some laughed in joy. Others gave prayers of thanksgiving.

Virginia just stared at the men who had come to save us.

"Are you from California?" she asked. "Or do you come from heaven?"

Chapter 11

The End of the Journey

Not everyone could leave with the first rescue party. Only the strongest were able to go.

On February 22, seven adults and sixteen children started out. Our family was among them.

But after only a few miles, Mama knew that Tommy wouldn't make it.

"How can I send him back alone?" she asked us. "But how can I let the rest of you go on without me?"

I was four days shy of my ninth birthday.
But I felt old beyond my years. I knew what
I had to do.

"You go ahead, Mama," I told her. "I'll
stay with Tommy."

Mama kissed me. She
promised me that Tommy
and I would be rescued.
Then she gave me the
handkerchief with
Grandma's lock of hair
inside.

"Keep this for me, my
brave girl," she whispered.
"Until we meet again."

Day by day, Tommy and I
waited to be rescued. Day by
day, he grew weaker.

The rescue party had left us some food.
But we had to make it last.

Who knew when we would make it out of the mountains? And would my brother still be alive when help came?

On March 1, I went out to the cabin roof to sit in the sun. As I looked toward the west, I couldn't believe my eyes.

Ten men were coming through the snow. The rescue party! Leading it was my own father!

I cried out. I stumbled back into the cabin.

I ran out to meet Papa. but I was so weak, I fell down. Tenderly, he gathered me up in his arms.

Papa and the other men passed out what food they had.

It was decided that three men would stay to take care of those still too weak to make it through the mountains. The other seven men would try to get as many children out as they could.

"We'll carry them if we have to," Papa said.

On March 3, Tommy and I started out on the last leg of our long, sad journey. Held tightly in my hands were my two treasures. One was the handkerchief Mama had given me. The other one was my doll.

"She's been with me all the way from Springfield," I told Papa proudly. "And now I shall carry her to California!"

Chapter

The Rest of the Story

Patty, Tommy, and James Reed were reunited with the rest of the family at Sutter's Fort. All of the Reed family survived the terrible journey to California. So did the Breen family.

William Eddy, who'd fought so bravely through the snow to bring help, lost both his wife and his children. He lived 11 years after the rescue.

Both Donner brothers and their wives died in the mountains. Three of their children died. Their other children were adopted. Two of them were taken in by James and Margaret Reed.

Four rescue parties went into the mountains. The last one left on April 20 with Lewis Keseberg. He was the last person left alive in the camp.

Eighty-one people were trapped in the mountains during the winter of 1846–47. It was the worst winter ever recorded in the Sierra Nevada.

Five women, fourteen children, and twenty-two men died of starvation and cold.

Truckee Lake was renamed Donner Lake. The mountain pass the pioneers struggled to cross was renamed Donner Pass.

Near the top of Donner Pass is Donner Memorial State Park. There is a museum there. This monument was built to honor the memory of the Donner party. Its base is 22 feet high. That is the exact height of the snow that fell that long winter.

The monument was dedicated on June 6, 1918. Virginia and Patty Reed were among the people present. They helped bury a time capsule that will be opened on June 6, 2018.

Dedication of the monument.
Patty Reed is second from the left, between the flags.

The Reed family settled in San Jose, California. James Reed made another fortune in the real estate business. He built a beautiful home.

Margaret Reed held on to the strength she found while trapped in the mountains. She was happy and healthy in her new life.

Virginia Reed married at age 17. She wrote about the trials of the Donner party in *Century Magazine.* Later, her article was turned into a book.

Patty Reed married at age 18. She had nine children.

A replica of Patty's doll is on display at Donner Memorial State Park. You can see her real doll at Sutter's Fort.

As Patty Reed said, many stories have been told about the Donner party. But the real story is about a group of ordinary people faced with terrible trouble.

Some of the people were broken by the trouble. But others showed great courage and concern for their fellow human beings.

Replica of Patty Reed's doll.